HER

KERRYN BEATTY

CURRENCY PRESS
The performing arts publisher

HotHouse
THEATRE

CURRENT THEATRE SERIES

First published in 2023
by Currency Press Pty Ltd,
PO Box 2287, Strawberry Hills, NSW, 2012, Australia
enquiries@currency.com.au
www.currency.com.au

in association with HotHouse Theatre

Typeset by Brighton Gray for Currency Press.
Cover features Kerry Beatty. Photo by Karen Donnelly.
Cover design, Luke Preston

Currency Press acknowledges the Traditional Owners of the Country on which
we live and work. We pay our respects to all Aboriginal and Torres Strait
Islander Elders, past and present.

A catalogue record for this
book is available from the
National Library of Australia

Contents

HER was commissioned and produced by Hot House Theatre. It was first performed at The Butter Factory Theatre, Albury Wodonga on 7 March 2023 with the following cast:

HER	Kerryn Beatty
YOUNG HER	Laura Trebley

Director, Karla Conway
Set & Costume Design, Imogen Keen
Composer & Sound Design, Helena Kernaghan
Lighting Design, Rob Scott
Movement Director, Ann-maree Ellis
Dramaturgy, Karla Conway
Stage Manager, Rebekah Gibbs
Production Manager, Kofi Isaacs
Producer, Beck Palmer

CHARACTERS

HER, regional woman in her 40s.

YOUNG HER, regional girl in her early teens.

NOTE

This symbol / denotes the start of the next line.

CONTENT ADVICE

This play has descriptions of animal slaughter.

DIVERSITY PLEDGE

I encourage anyone producing and casting this work to consider performers and creatives from diverse backgrounds, especially where a character's ethnic or cultural background, age, sexuality, gender or disability need not be specified.

This play text went to press before the end of rehearsals and may differ from the play as performed.

SCENE 1

After.

The stage is misty/foggy with low light.

HER *is onstage. A red and green dragon delivers* YOUNG HER *to the stage.*

YOUNG HER *stalks the stage, and eventually finds herself in her corner.*

YOUNG HER: They send me out to check the traps. Get the rabbits. Get them before something else does. Get them out of the trap before they chew their legs off and damage their fur. Always have the twenty-two in case. Stop. Don't move. Don't move.

  Sound of a heartbeat.

Don't. Move. Can you see it? See its eyes? Looking at us. Keep your eyes on it …

  A gun fires.

It's on the move. Half its face blown off. Shit! Gotta kill it. No bullets left. Corner it at the fence lines. My hands are too small … I want to go back to the house to get more bullets. That'll take too long. It has to be done. I cry with every whack! Can't leave it. It won't be able to eat. Whack! It will die anyway. Whack! It's better this way. Whack! It dies and I go up my hill.

  Heartbeat stops.

HER: Nothing.

  There are thoughts. Of you. Oxygen—that isn't nothing.

  In

  HER *struggles to breathe without pain.*

  Out

  Dust fairies. Wings. Don't hide them. That's her corner. You'll get caught in her spinning. You would get caught. Your wings are …

  Puff of dragon smoke.

Birds? Left too.

  Yellow eyes pecking.

I'm such an arsehole.
Ready.
In

HER *inhales.*

Ouch. A bit longer.
Can I shower today? Fuck it hurts. Heavy. Alone. Pulsing. Red.
No-one comes. I smell. Foul, breath, garlic, chicken soup. I'm the same. Am I? Why am I? They fondled, foraged, tore at me. There's someone else in there.
Do I feel different? I look different.
I see no-one. Hear nothing. Say … Alone.
He doesn't come. They did. I cried. He's doing. This is my new.
I can't speak.
I can't read.
I can't shower.
I can't breathe.
I can't stand.
I can't …
I am heavy black.
Filled with black.
Spewing black. I shouldn't be.

SCENE 2

Before.

HER: I'm in my forties. I still don't know … I've got kids. I've got him. Jesus! I live here. I'm tired.
YOUNG HER: A pack lives here. Of boys. Catching blowies. Crawling the walls. Punching. Noisy. I keep moving.
HER: I was meant to leave.
YOUNG HER: I'll leave here one day.
HER: Tried travel, tried uni, tried singing.
Tried trucking, tried farming, tried acting.
Tried yoga, tried being vegetarian, tried being sober.
Tried parenting. Can't give that up.
'Mum. Mummmmmmmmmmmmmm.'

Yes?

'There's no food. Can we have a lunch order?'

Really? We live on a (fucking) farm.

YOUNG HER: The pack eat a lot.

HER: 'Mummmmmmm.'

Just make your lunch.

'Mum, she swore at me.'

'I did not!'

Can you sort that please? I'm on the loo! For fuck's sake.

I love being active. Moving through the universe. None of my plans … Get out, act, sing, be…

YOUNG HER *is dancing and singing.*

YOUNG HER: I want to be a singer and a dancer.

HER: … a backup dancer like the ones in a Frank Sinatra movie.

YOUNG HER: They see me and chase me.

HER: That's not a plan, for you.

YOUNG HER: I am fast. I could be an athlete. If I had trainers.

HER: Just keep moving. In a car. On a train. On a plane, out of here. Moving so fast you can't see yourself.

YOUNG HER: I run, fast, trip on a broken fence and land in the mud. They all laugh.

HER: My days are normal.

YOUNG HER: I want to / yell

HER: Yell at the kids to get them ready, get me ready. On the treadmill.

YOUNG HER: I climb to the top of the hill and sit on my rock under the big tree and hide.

HER: From farm to little town, to big town.

To childcare, to school, to work.

Finish work, pick up from school.

Drop at dance and sport.

Pick up from dance, sport and childcare and back to the farm.

'Mummmmmm what's for dinner?'

Here we go!

Can someone do the watering?

'I did it last time.'

Just fucking do it. You are so lazy.

YOUNG HER: Can't be lazy.

HER: To work, to cook, to clean.

YOUNG HER: The rock lizard watches me.

HER: To help with homework.

YOUNG HER: My green and red rock dragon. I pat it.

HER: A few drinks. Take the edge off … this reality.

YOUNG HER: It grows wings, grows big. Grows greener and we fly and breathe red.

HER: Off to bed. Normal, right?

YOUNG HER: They can't get me up here.

HER: But I am tired. All the time. Like, rest doesn't work.

> Am I lazy?
> Maybe I am.
> I didn't try at all.

SCENE 3

Before.

HER: Hey. Yeah, we're free. A barbecue sounds great. What can I bring? Of course, I can make something. A salad? Yeah!

He drops me and the kids and everything else at the barbecue. He'll come back later. He has stuff to do. I take everything.

Arms full of kids' stuff, cheese platters, drinks. The salad!

'Is he working again?'

'We haven't seen him in ages.'

'I don't know how he does it all.'

'He's so good. You couldn't do better.'

SCENE 4

Before.

HER *is plucking her chin hairs.* YOUNG HER *is checking out her knee warts.*

HER: Self love. I'll do some of that. These tags gotta go, I mean, I'm not vain!

YOUNG HER: I wish I had long hair,

HER: But sight issues, surely.

YOUNG HER: … and no warts.

HER: From farm to little town to big town. Skin tag man talks at me.

'You need to keep up with your checks. Women reach a certain age.'

Bloody hell! I'm not that old.

YOUNG HER: Mum says spit on your warts when you first wake up.

HER: These old lady warts. Can you just / get rid of them.

YOUNG HER: Gets rid of them.

HER: 'I will. But go and see your specialist!'

From farm to little town to big town. Again.

The sound of a bicuspid aortic (broken) heart fills the space. Image of the aortic valve pumping projected ...

I lie on the bed. The gown drapes loosely across my bareness. I try and look relaxed, cool, in control. The room darkens. The sounds come on, and the screens come alive. I look down, the gown has shifted, my breasts bare, and hanging low. Kids. I forgot to pluck. Glad the lights are low. I wonder if you can laser there. Who do I ask about that? I don't want to cover myself in case I look uncool. You know. Love your body and all that.

YOUNG HER: Vanity is a sin.

HER: I think I saw you last time. Six years? Shit. Time flies.

Beat.

So ... how's your kids? They'd be in high school then?

He nods.

Beat.

It sounds like a heart to me.

He just gets up and walks out.

Then the doors open, and a white coat followed by a sea of blue strides into this darkened room and surrounds me. Clipboards at the ready. 'Listening; a bicuspid aortic regurgitation.' White coat looks down at me lying there, and ... not a word. Turns and walks out followed by the blue sea.

Awkward silence.

From big town to little town to farm. And the broken fence lines.

'Mummmmmmmmmm, why are you late? I've got dance rehearsals.'

You are so lucky to have rehearsals.

YOUNG HER: I would love singing lessons.

HER: 'Here we go.' Mimics one little smart arse.
YOUNG HER: I ask Mum.
HER: You are getting way more opportunities than I ever did.
YOUNG HER: Don't be silly, she says.
HER: Fucking spoilt brats actually if you really want to know. So bloody well appreciate it you fucking little shit heads.

    I don't say it out loud. I never do.

SCENE 5

Before.

HER *is starting to get the sense that something is wrong with her health.*

HER: I cut the chicken.
    With the butcher's knife.
    I look at the knife.
YOUNG HER: A gun is outside, leaning against the kitchen wall.
HER: I look at them.
YOUNG HER: I pick it up and point it. At them.
HER: / It would be so easy to stop this.
YOUNG HER: It would be so easy to stop this.
    Mum talks me down.
HER: I stop using the knife.
    My hands can break the chicken.
    I go and see someone.
    I am bored. Fancy! Mothering is …
YOUNG HER: Don't listen to them.
HER: Scream

    YOUNG HER *screams.*

On and on in my head
    It won't stop.
    I stop, unbuckle it, and throw.
    On the side of the road.
    Someone else will pick it up.
    I drive away.
YOUNG HER: I go up my hill.
HER: The screaming, it stays.

SCENE 6

Before.

HER: Past that broken fence. From farm to little town to big town. Back to those rooms for results. I hope I don't have to get my boobs out again.

YOUNG HER: Mum takes me to the doctor in little town.

HER: Hi. How are you? I'm here to see the specialist. Thank you.

YOUNG HER: He likes to listen to my beats. Smile, says Mum.

HER: I go into the waiting room. There's always a weight in the waiting room. The other waiters look to see who the new waiter is. I scan the room looking for the one. There's always one who wants to chat, or sit too close, or smells of perfume over unwashed. They're all old in here. I wonder how long they've been waiting.

I sit and look out the only window. And hear the tap tap of the trapped lonely blowie. 'Open the window. Let in some fresh air.' That's what Mum would say. It's painted shut.

I close my hand around the blowie to take it outside. And just as I open the door my name is called, gently, by a handsome man with a kind face. Fuck! I release the blowie and the door closes.

I turn back and smile. I go in. I smile some more. Kind face directs me to the chair right opposite. I sit down smiling. By this time my face hurts. No desk between us. Our knees almost touching. Hmmmm.

YOUNG HER: Doctor in little town sends me to the doctor in big town. He likes to listen to my beats too.

HER: My old doctor had a big desk.

YOUNG HER: He's got a big desk with big chairs.

HER: The bigger the better. To keep you distant I suppose. Kind face leans in.

YOUNG HER: I keep smiling.

HER: 'How are you feeling?'

I'm great! Fine. I mean, I'm tired. I've got kids.

Kind face takes my arm and checks my pulse. Shit! I hope it's not racing.

How about this weather? Not a cloud.
'Any shortness of breath?'

HER *talks under her breath.*

Well, possibly at the moment.
No. Should there be?
Kind face still has hold of my arm.
YOUNG HER: Doctor in big town sends me to the big city. It's a long way. They have a machine there.
HER: 'I'm sending you to the city.'
YOUNG HER: There's no machines in little town.
HER: 'You are in severe heart failure.'

Beat.

No. I feel fine.
YOUNG HER: There's no machines in big town.
HER: It's never been a bother.
YOUNG HER: And the machine doesn't work when we are in the big city.
HER: I can't be a bother.
YOUNG HER: So, we go home again.
HER: 'You need open heart surgery.'

Beat.

YOUNG HER: Whenever I go to the doctor they love to listen to my beats.
HER: Look at me, I'm great. I'm doing great. It's just a double beat.
YOUNG HER: I will listen to my own beats.
HER: I can feel it working. It's pounding in there. I've got kids. I'm a bit busy.
YOUNG HER: The sheep hang on the veranda.
HER: Death I've thought about.
YOUNG HER: They need cutting up.
HER: Not by you. Power tools.
YOUNG HER: We take the sheets off, check for flies. I have to hold the legs.
HER: Who will hold mine?
YOUNG HER: The boys do the sawing.
HER: Cracking ribs.

YOUNG HER: Meat dust falls in my hair.

HER: Will they cover my hair?

YOUNG HER: Cut the maggots out.

HER: He leads me to the door.

    'How'd you go?'

    Yeah, great. He's lovely.

    'That'll be a hundred and eighty dollars for today thanks. So, what's on for the rest of your day?'

    I prefer the big desk.

SCENE 7

Before.

YOUNG HER: I follow the pack along the top of the creek bank. We are up really high. You gotta stay away from the edge or you get pushed. There's a rabbit sitting on the edge. Its ears turn to us. Run little bunny! It stays. It's got pussy eyes, pussy mouth, pussy nose. One steps back, lines it up, runs, and … kicks … it lands, snap! On the other side. Can't waste the bullets.

HER: I am outside at my car, call him. What have I done? What have I been doing? He comes from farm to little town to big town.

YOUNG HER: I hang at the back of the pack.

HER: To find me. Hold me.

YOUNG HER: Seeing nothing, hearing nothing, smelling nothing.

HER: I can't see. My tears. My breath, short. I retch. I sit in the street of big town and wonder at the spring sun, can't feel it. Look at the birds, can't hear them. See the cars going by. Do I step off the edge?

YOUNG HER: I like it when they can't feel anymore.

HER: When you kill something. See it dead after you whack it. There's nothing in the eyes.

YOUNG HER: Wobbly jelly that can't feel.

HER: Looks like jelly.

YOUNG HER: You can't eat a rabbit with myxo.

    Beat.

HER: I could go anywhere I want.

YOUNG HER: You didn't.

HER: Too scared
YOUNG HER: Too scared?
HER: Still Scared.
YOUNG HER: Still scared?
HER: Got your whole life ahead of you …
YOUNG HER: You can go anywhere you want.
HER: Too old. Too late.
YOUNG HER: Be brave.

Beat.

HER: From big town to little, I see the one tree that sits on top of the big hill. The sun shining on its branches and the rock glistening underneath.
YOUNG HER: I go up my hill to my rock, my lizards, my critters.

Dragon shadow appears.

HER: You can't see it when you get into little town. Little town is in a hole. Climb out of little town and head to the farm. The clouds are heaving ready to dump on the …
Same bends, same neighbour, same drive pattern.
Same fucked driveway. Potholes ready to fill but can't get to.
Same broken fence lines …
When are you going to fix the fences?
'It'll happen. It'll come. Be patient.'
Mum makes.
Chicken soup, pumpkin soup, lamb shanks, steak and kidney, apple tart, soda bread, Irish stew, rabbit stew.
YOUNG HER: Rabbit stew. Again!

Beat.

HER: What are you going to do when you come back?
Eat! Pluck my bits. Fucking hair removal. I'm not vain! Yeah, right. Get someone to do that in case …
Get the good photos of me out and burn the shit ones. He likes the photos I hate. We see each other … do we even see each other? There's a really nice one of me in a silver dress, I looked great.
'Is that you Mum? Wow! You were young … and pretty. Did you want to be a dancer too?'

SCENE 8

Before.

HER *smile is waning.*

HER: From farm to little town to big town to coffee shop. It's a double shots day. To big city. He takes me to see power tools man. The cutter. In the big city. We wait in another waiting room.

YOUNG HER: The blowflies love banging their heads against the glass.

HER: It's high up in the big city.

YOUNG HER: Why do they come in and then want to get out?

HER: A high office, in a high building, on a high hill.

YOUNG HER: The boys catch the blowies.

HER: Up so high the birds nesting on the window ledge watch us watching them.

YOUNG HER: Tie cotton around their necks and lead them around. Until their heads drop off.

HER: Cutter is small. Mini cutter. But has a big stare, and a big desk. Warm hands, no small talk, just the facts.

'You also have an aneurysm. You have a choice.'

Do I?

'Of heart valves. Porcine, bovine, mechanical. Or human donor valve for the Ross procedure … if you're healthy enough. We switch out your damaged aortic valve with your pulmonary valve and put a donor valve into your pulmonary position. When we crack you open and see your insides we will know what to do. We need to wait for a donor match. Please sign here.'

Fresh flesh … what the … something, someone has to die for me to live?

The dragon presence is felt. A gunshot sounds.

YOUNG HER: Shit!

HER: Pig, cow, clicking clock, bionic woman, someone else, holy shit … this is real!

YOUNG HER: I run along the fence lines. Which way did it run?

HER: I could be a pig.

This little piggy went to market.

This little piggy stayed though.

YOUNG HER: There's a hole in the fence and bits of fur hanging on the barbed wire. There is soft poo.

HER: I don't want this.

YOUNG HER: No! There's blood on the rocks covering the sparkles.

HER: 'Do you want to live?'

'Yes. She does.'

'The heart works until it doesn't.'

Pig, cow, human. Will his hands fit? I wonder if they have killed. Will he cut out the shit and leave me hollow. No blood under his fingernails. I bet he has to manicure. He could jump right into my chest. Forage, saw out the flesh stench. All of mini cutter with his mini chainsaw.

YOUNG HER: Where did it go? The spiders are spinning their night webs.

HER: My legs want to run.

YOUNG HER: I keep running the ley lines.

HER: I always want to run.

YOUNG HER: Looking. Over the edge.

HER: Keep moving. In a car, on a train, on a plane. Outta here. So fast I can't see who I've become.

YOUNG HER: The sun is down. Breath is hard to get.

HER: Go home and we will call you when we find a match.

YOUNG HER: I have to go. The pack is howling.

HER: We're on our way, Mum. See you in a few hours. How are the kids? I hope they were good. I know … they're always good for you. Umm yeah. Got to wait for a donor match. Something about a Ross procedure. I know. There's a lot worse off than me. I am thankful Mum. See you soon.

SCENE 9

Before.

HER *is breathless.*

HER: From big city to drive thru. Coffee won't cut it. To big town, to servo, to little town, to home. Home to the farm. The fucking farm. The fucking farmhouse where they are all hanging on the walls. Where I will. Will I hang on the wall? Talons on the wall beside the grandparents. Wait. Waiting is not doing. Fuck. I can't. What do I do? I stop. I see. The things that aren't done … things I haven't done. The clothesline is vacant. I can't even hang the washing.

YOUNG HER: I hold the ducks upside down over the bowl after the boys cut their heads off.

HER: Look normal.

YOUNG HER: I hold them by their feet.

HER: Act normal.

YOUNG HER: Until the blood stops and they stop.

HER: Do the same, but not the same. Get up. That's hard now. No breath life left. Help the kids. Help them get ready. I need to help. Because he can't do it like me. He does farm to little town to big town. To childcare to school to work. Finish work, pick up from school drop at sport and dance. Pick up from sport and dance and childcare and back to the farm. And I … complain. He's late. Dinner is late. It's not done how I like. For fuck's sake!!

YOUNG HER: I take the bowl to Mum, and she makes pudding.

HER: Mum arrives.

'I've made some dinner. And I'll hang out the washing.'

YOUNG HER: The boys hang the ducks on the clothesline.

HER: We have to wait.

YOUNG HER: After the slaughter.

HER: Until / all the ducks are in a row.

YOUNG HER: All the ducks are in a row.

HER: Right tissue match, right cutter, right theatre.

YOUNG HER: Wash them in detergent. Pull out the down and make the pillows.

Her's phone rings with a quack quack tone.

HER: 'Hello. It's Margaret from Mr Mad's rooms.'

What is it with the doctors versus the misters?

'We've come across the most beautiful piece of tissue. It will be just perfect for you. It's coming all the way from Western Australia.'

I wonder if I'll become a Freo supporter.

YOUNG HER: When I grow up, I'll buy food from the shops.

HER: My kids want me to read them *Bambi*.

'They've come a long way in medicine,' says Mum.

Pack stuff, label stuff. This time I may not come back. But I always come back.

YOUNG HER: When I grow up.

HER: I've got to get them ready.

YOUNG HER: I'll get singing lessons in the big town.

HER: She loves my stuff. My shoes, my clothes, the silver dress. She will grow into them. They will all grow.

YOUNG HER: When I grow up, I'll get dance lessons in the big city.

HER: 'Most heart attacks happen on Mondays Mum.'

'Will they fix your love heart?'

From farm to little town to big town to coffee shop. But I want a drink. To big city. This is a long time together, just the two of us. What to talk about. The closest person to me and … nothing. He's driving. He's doing. He's never waited.

YOUNG HER: When I grow up, I can leave here.

HER: I've never screamed. Outwards.

HER *is singing along to a song on the radio while He is driving.*

I'm in love now with your kindness it's the bigness of your … heart.

I'm in love with the way your hands help everyone.

I'm in love with the way you listen and slowly smile.

I'm in love with the way you smile at me and really see.

I'm in love with the way you make your endless cups of tea.

I'm in love.

It's good to see your happy head bopping around the place.

I like the way you're slow to smile but the first to grin.

I'm in love with the way you do things for me.

Just the way I like it, I hold your face now.

Just the way I like it, lips sweet to taste.

Cos I'm in love, love, love, I'm in love.

Before.

HER: It's dark. We haven't slept. He holds me all night in this hospital bed. You know how small these beds are? He ain't small. I'm small. Meant to be smaller. They give me drugs to sleep, but they don't work. I want to feel, everything.

    YOUNG HER *is preparing to load the twenty-two rifle.*

YOUNG HER: They sit there on the wall above the TV. Bullets on the shelf next to them.

    HER *is on the phone.*

HER: I'm a voyeur, not a contributor. But I post to announce …

    Let people know that he could be on his own. There'd be someone who could love him. Sit with his silence. Learn his eye language. Wait for the pearl.

YOUNG HER: We are made to clean the barrels. Get the specs out of the shafts.

HER: Sat up there. Looked, listened, smelt, felt.

YOUNG HER: Everything seems so far away.

HER: I said goodbye.

YOUNG HER: When you look down the barrel.

HER: Waves, memories, flurries in the gut.

    'That's the eggs.' He says.

    No, it's more that that. You love it here. I tried. Too many … memories.

    'Some good.'

    Undercurrent of fear.

    'Get a grip and tear it out.'

YOUNG HER: The rabbits suffer if you don't get them in the head.

HER: Will this tear it out? Leave it behind?

YOUNG HER: All the critters suffer if you leave them injured.

HER: It's here in this. Seeping into my pores. I don't know how to stop it. Oil slick stuff. Can't take it off. It won't wash off.

    'Use soap.'

    He's so fucking practical!

YOUNG HER: There's blood in my undies. I try and hide it. Other things bleed Mum! Not me!

HER: I look at him lying there. Resting. Holding me. He has always held me tightly. I tell him I don't need you. I don't need you anymore. And I nearly believe it.

   They come; they surround me. Watching. I scrub all my bits. Under my small boobs. I put myself in an open at the front gown.

YOUNG HER: Mum says it's normal. Just what happens. And don't leave your undies there.

HER: I put myself on the trolley. They put machines on me. No words, no eyes, they don't see me.

YOUNG HER: My blood is boiling. My blood is on fire. I am spewing fire.

HER: They wheel me out into the long corridor of forever fluoros. Towards the brighter lights. Not the lights of my dreams.

YOUNG HER: I need to put the gun down.

HER: Nurse wipes my cheeks.

YOUNG HER: It's hard to pull the trigger.

HER: Knock out man sees me awake. All that red wine. These drugs won't work.

YOUNG HER: When they are looking at you.

HER: Do you see me?

YOUNG HER: We talk about Russian Roulette.

HER: Ten, nine, eight. There's the … reds and greens.

YOUNG HER: Seven, six, five … don't look.

HER: Dragon! I never wanted to kill anything.

   A gunshot sounds.

SCENE 11

During.

HER *holds her heart in her hands as they fix her.* YOUNG HER *dances and sings softly.*

HER: The water flows clear. Crystal. I see the critters underneath, magnified. Young eyes looking up, out and away and seeing me.

YOUNG HER: And me seeing them.

HER: We live in both worlds.

YOUNG HER: I need to come up for air.

HER: Not me. I merge into the water. The mud and blood wash off. Flow with the current. Leeches and yabbies face the current, swish and wiggle. No fight. Their dead eyes close and I close mine and free fall into the depths. I go, I go, I go.

YOUNG HER: My red and green dragon picks me up and out, into the air, I breathe.

HER: And I can breathe. I fill up with heat, holding on. Never to let it go again.

YOUNG HER: Running along the river of dreams. Big girls come and play, and I like it. Their hair long with ribbons. I see her dancing on the green and red. Dust fairies wearing dresses. Webs dangle over my chest. Sun shines on the rocks. The magic revealed. Of the trees, the grass, the rocks. We soar above the clouds and see everything sparkle.

The sun chinks in the cloud. We follow the light line over the land. Along the creek, to the top of the hill. And hear the trees talking in their whispers. The quartz holding solid in the land. The rocks glistening and cleansing the water as it rolls over them.

I love it.

HER: I love it here.

YOUNG HER: I love it here, I love it here!

HER: I love being here.

YOUNG HER: Dancing with the breeze.

HER: Gossamer in the sun, patterns I know. Spinning their webs, silk healing. Webs precise, symmetrical, just like them.

YOUNG HER: My body hair sprouts.

HER: Webs. I am full of spiders. Full of silk healing.

YOUNG HER: The birds sing. I listen to their cries, their laughter, their chatter. I love their song. I mimic and sing with them, they mimic me.

HER: We sing in tune.

YOUNG HER: They see me. They all see me. I dip and twirl, nearly fall off.

HER: And they laugh with me.

YOUNG HER: I know how to now. My dragons know how too.

HER: I watch the creek flow through my veins. The leeches travel cleansing my blood. Wildflowers. Tiny specs of colour. Lyrebirds in the hills I hear and see. This is what I fell for. This is who I am. He has always seen me. I lost myself.

The dragon breathes fire.

The little one takes off her trainer wheels by herself. Rides and falls. Tries and falls. Puts one wheel back on and rides sideways. Her ways.

YOUNG HER: She holds my heart in her hands.

> HER *is taken off the bypass machine.* HER *heart is plugged back into* HER.

SCENE 12

After.

ICU. HER *on stage alone directly after surgery.*

HER: I open my eyes. No-one. White coats are … room beeping.

Blood on my toes. Wash it off little piggy. This little piggy went to market. Tell me what you did? You jumped in. This little piggy stayed. Heparin. Get out prick. Not by the hair of my chinny chin chin.

I am alone. The critters. He doesn't come. I see no flowers, no-one. Dead things. Am I dead? Did they cut me up too?

Where are the flowers spilling over the cabinets? I could hitchhike outta here if I was a boy. He doesn't see. I know. Her wasn't there. The leeches suck at my scabs.

He's looking at his hands. Am I a pig? No. Machine? No. Someone else? Someone else. So … I go for Freo.

The frogs chatter to the tadpoles. The ones I caught, I let them go before they grow. I wish they let me go. The crow looks at me with yellow eyes. It's not frightened of me. Sitting there eating a mandarin. Pecking out the flesh and leaving it hollow. We all need vitamin C. The boys shoot it and hang it on the fence. I ask the nurse to shoot me.

I'll come to you and your spinning.

All white and light. Reds and greens on white.

White everything. I am light and naked.

I slip back to my dragon.

SCENE 13

After.

HER *has a psychotic episode on the ward. The dragon comes out of the walls.*
HER *is clawing her way back to her dragon. Claws her way back to* HER.
HER *absorbs the blood transfusion. The blood looks black.*

SCENE 14

After psychosis.

HER: I open my eyes in a room on my own. My dragon is gone. I can
    see … but …

I'm here, black ice freezing me.

I'm searching. There's vast land between us, uncovered. And
this is all because I …

I'm here without you.

Water spills down my cheeks when I swallow my pills. Spit
spills down my cheeks.

I don't want to wet the bed. I have to get up. I have wet the bed.
No noise.
No clock.
No music.
No radio.
No flowers.
No-one.

I stare out the window. I have time and days and days of doing
nothing. You can't be lazy. You've got to be doing. Do it properly
or don't do it at all.

I sweep the garden.
Prune my face.
Dodge the bees.
Run to the river.
Climb a mountain.
Speak to Ireland, in my bones.
Go back to the womb.

SCENE 15

After.

HER: He brings me my going home outfit. It's not the silver dress.

I am gifted a bag of pills. I smile and say thank you. All kinds of colours dance in my hand.

From the high on the hospital, out of the big city, up the open road. Look at all the speed cameras, and a new Bunnings. He looks at me sideways. Have they always been there?

I saw our neighbours at the hospital. He looks at me sideways. What about the nurse with the pig needle. He looks at me sideways.

'The medicine. It didn't suit you. The city is too far away, but they are all asking after you.'

But you weren't there. You had to be with the kids?! There were no flowers. No-one was there. It was the stay in the hospital where I wanted to see people. To soften the fluoro lights and drown out the beeps.

He's driving. He talks. I look at … This Dalí painting? Familiar but … I don't know who I am in this.

I just wanted someone to be with me. I just wanted someone to see me. I just wanted someone … I don't tell him about the dragons. I close my eyes and breathe into this new.

Beat.

I am home and the kids find a leveret and are so excited. I remember I have to be for them. Be Mum for them. So, I tell them a story.

When I was your age this place was full of rabbits. Then something happened to them. They all got myxomatosis and died. The hares moved in. The hare mum, well, she scatters her babies around to different spots. She doesn't have a home for them. She only sees them twice a day for a feed. That's it for her parenting.

The kids go find their dad. They don't like my story.

I scramble to the top of the hill. To my rock and the big tree. I sit quietly in the shade. Looking in the cracks, waiting. It doesn't come. It's gone. Like me, it's gone. How do I find it?

Beat.

Can you do all you want to do? Cutter asks me on my check up. I'd never been asked that before. I'd never thought about what I want to do. The smiling got in the way. I throw away the pills. I want to see and feel and breathe and drive.

SCENE 16

After.

Another barbecue.

HER: 'It will be good for you to see people. Just for a little while.'
Who? The people who didn't come and see me?
'You wear it like a badge of honour,' said one of the ladies.
I take to wearing high of the neck, turtle variety. They don't want to hear or see the unsavoury. The clothes I packed in boxes stay there. They aren't me anymore.
'Don't be intense. Keep it light babe.'
But I find the dark bits more interesting. He doesn't laugh.
I drive to the barbecue. The kids run off. He takes everything. Arms full of kid's stuff, cheese platters, drinks. Where's the salad? I walk in with nothing. And it feels good. He goes to the shed. I see the ladies in the kitchen. But I go and sit in the paddock. It's rich, loved, fenced! I shrink to see the blue flowers, precise, not big, whole.
I take a deep breath …
'Hi! We haven't seen you in ages. How's things?'
'How's he been coping without you?'
'By himself with the kids. He's so good.'
'You couldn't do better.'
The ladies keep spewing, the sun is going down and the reds and greens are calling.

HER *comes face to face with* YOUNG HER.

YOUNG HER: I'm in love now with your kindness it's the bigness of your heart.
I'm in love with the way your hands help everyone.
I'm in love with the way you listen.
I'm in love with the way you smile at me and really see.

I'm in love with the way you do things so beautifully.
I'm in love with the way you need to make me grin.
I'm in love with the way you stand firm in a storm.
Stand your ground.
I'm in love with you.

Beat.

HER: I listened to myself. I am not smiling. Not anymore.

The whole stage screams.

I need to learn to breathe fire again.
I leave the barbecue.
I leave the farm.
I leave him.

SCENE 17

After.

HER *and* YOUNG HER *are cocooned in the webs of silk healing.*

HER: I put my whole body into the thickest web. It closes in around me.
The web stops my bleeding. I always thought the house was kept
together by webs. I'll come to you and your spinning.

I miss the garden.
Seeing their faces,
dodging the bees.
My heart says …
I go,

Run with the river.
Climb my mountain.
Breath Ireland, in my bones.
And I go home.

EPILOGUE

The dragon delivers HER *to the top of the hill.*

HER: He's down there fixing the fence lines.
New wire holds us together.
I am up here, looking.
Like so many eyes before, seeing.
Green paddocks, blue hills, red sunset.
Horizons of forever.
Scars leading out made by us and the critters, going and coming
back.

The wind. Can be ferocious.
Baby spiders hang onto their webs. Some get caught in the long
grass.
Others fly right up into the sky, twinkle in the sunlight and float
away to other lands.
Or get eaten by the birds.
Some return to this land to spin new webs.
A light breeze moves through my cheek hairs and my thoughts.
YOUNG HER: I catch my hand on the barbed wire. Mum rubs salt on it.
We go and find the biggest and thickest web. I put the cut hand into
the webs. Keeping it still as the webs close in around the cut.
HER: The rabbits are all gone. The house looks small down there.

I watch her climb these rocks to the top of the hill.
The silk, silver dress spun her way.
We stand on the power nodes and look at the ley of the land.
Talk about the magic. The reds and the greens.
Put our arms out. The wind catches our wings and takes us.
Into the blazing sunset, over the verdant paddocks and up into
the white clouds.

She is wise yet knows little. Of the world in which she lives.
She is brave in her world, she is living, that we cannot see.
And we love her.

THE END

HotHouse
THEATRE

HotHouse Theatre presents a world premiere production.

HER
by Kerryn Beatty

CAST

HER	Kerryn Beatty
YOUNG HER	Laura Trebley

CREATIVE

DIRECTOR	Karla Conway
SET & COSTUME	Imogen Keen
COMPOSER | SOUND	Helena Kernaghan
LIGHTING	Rob Scott
MOVEMENT DIRECTOR	Ann-maree Ellis
DRAMATURGY	Karla Conway

PRODUCTION

PRODUCER	Beck Palmer
PRODUCTION MANAGER	Kofi Isaacs
STAGE MANAGER	Bek Gibbs
RIGGER	Simon Yates
AERIAL CONSULTANT	Lauren Shepherd
PRODUCTION ASSISTANT	Hannah Mulholland
PHOTOGRAPHY	Karen Donnelly | Karla Conway
GRAPHIC DESIGN	Luke Preston

HER was commissioned and produced by HotHouse Theatre.

Acknowledgment to Country

HotHouse Theatre recognises Aboriginal and Torres Strait Islander peoples as the First Peoples of this land.

We acknowledge the traditional custodians of the lands upon which HotHouse Theatre stands and pay our respect to the Ancestors, Elders and storytellers, who hold the memories, traditions and cultural knowledge of this place.

We recognise the historical impact of the past endures, and we embrace our responsibility to listen deeply, care for Country, and respect the resilience and wisdom of the world's oldest continuing culture, as we journey forward together.

KERRYN BEATTY
Playwright | HER

HER began as *Heart Story*, a monologue about my experience with having open heart surgery. This monologue became a finalist in Solo, a writing competition led by La Trobe University and Write Around the Murray.

I was kindly pushed along by close friends to expand on that monologue and as I had written a few songs over the years, the idea of *Heart Story* as a song cycle presented itself.

Heart Story had its first creative development through HotHouse Theatre's CELSIUS: Independent Theatre program, where I was fortunate to muster these talented people: Alyson Evans, Helena Kernaghan and Suzanne Pereira. We explored the concept and how the story would be told.

As writing progressed it was resonating with those around me. My chest had been sawn open and exposed, so why not talk about it, expose myself further?

HER was being revealed.

HER is a story of being female, growing up in a regional setting and what expectations, real or imagined, are placed on us. Of how hard parenting can be, how hard being a partner is. It highlights the compromises that come with being in a couple, a family. It exposes how women are often treated versus men when there is a crisis in the family. *HER* questions what she wants in relation to what is expected of her.

While *HER* is a deeply personal story, it is a work of fiction based in fact. The woman in *HER* is me, but maybe she is you too?

Kerryn Beatty is a singer/songwriter, actor and playwright based in Albury. A graduate of Swinburne University (Performing Arts), Kerryn has developed an eclectic career across theatre and music. Alongside her performance practice, Kerryn also works as producer for Murray River Fine Music.

Kerryn has had a long association with HotHouse Theatre and its predecessor MRPG. For HotHouse Theatre: *A Midsummer Night's Dream, Burn, Body of Desire, Embers – Anniversary Reading, Unprecedented* (Creative Development), *Last Summer* (Creative Development). For Swinburne: Art of Success. For AlburyCity: Hidden Cinema.

She is currently working on a new concept album, a companion piece to *HER. HER* is Kerryn's first commission by HotHouse as playwright and she is thrilled to be premiering this work at her home company.

KARLA CONWAY
Director | Dramaturg

HER is one of the most beautiful and vulnerable pieces of writing I have come across in decades.

It is audacious and bold in the questions it raises and the conversation it is opening, whilst being subversive, poetic, and lyrical. Like the character *HER*, the journey of this play has been one of evolution and transformation.

hearing the first scenes that Kerryn wrote back in 2019, I was struck by this strong, instinctive, and specifically regional voice coming off the page. The text was evocative, imagistic, and theatrical, with a divine rhythm and cadence, merging the best of her lyric writing style as a singer/songwriter with her compelling personal narrative, to produce a symphony of the human spirit in all its beauty and its complexity.

HER is an everywoman. She is our mothers. She is us. She is our daughters. Regardless of our generation, from the moment we are born we are being moulded, shaped, influenced, controlled, and sculpted by the multitude of forces around us. The process of growing up takes us from the purest essence of ourselves, on a journey to find our purpose while negotiating an avalanche of expectations from every direction. An inevitable odyssey – it is most impossible not to lose some part of yourself in the process.

Through facing her own mortality *HER* is awakened to the structures that have been at play in her life, cultural conditioning, gender, farm life, social and familial expectations on women regarding career, family, motherhood. She has become unrecognisable to herself.

The arrival of YOUNG HER provokes us all to think about our inner child, the younger version of ourselves that arises in our memories. Facing the child we were, as the person we've become, brings into sharp perspective, the winding paths our lives have taken. No matter our age, we have the opportunity to be renewed. To find our way back to ourselves. *HER* reminds us we are the sum of all our experiences, to embrace them fully is to know myself.

is also to understand tomorrow is a new day and the best of us is always, yet to come.

Karla Conway is an award-winning director, dramaturg, theatre-maker and current Artistic Director & CEO of HotHouse Theatre.

She has created numerous innovative works as a theatre maker, including site-specific interactive and live gaming works for the National Library and the National Gallery of Australia; and has collaborated with artists and companies across the country including in works for: Sydney Opera House, Black Swan State Theatre Company (WA), The Street (ACT), Action Transport Theatre (UK), Canberra Youth Theatre, Warehouse Circus, Long Cloud Youth Theatre (NZ) and the Academy of Interactive Entertainment.

Recent works include: *Those Who Fall in Love Like Anchors Dropped Upon the Ocean Floor* (Finegan Kruckemeyer), world premieres - *All the Shining Lights* (Brendan Hogan), *HER* (Kerryn Beatty), *Unprecedented* (Campion Decent) and *This Is Your City – The Live Game* (Karla Conway, Rachel McNamara, Nick Stannard). Karla is a passionate advocate for the development of artists and new Australian work. She has been resident Dramaturg for Australian Dance Party (ADP) and Warehouse Circus for many years and is thrilled to be supporting the development of new works now from regional Australia.

LAURA TREBLEY
YOUNG HER

Laura was a full-time dance student throughout her high school years, completing her contemporary dance training and VCE both in 2021. Laura performed in multiple productions with Projection Dance Company and some highlights were *Forte and Intent*, plus *eMerge* - a collaboration with the Flying Fruit Fly Circus. At 17, Laura interned in stage management, choreography and dramaturgy with Projection Dance Company.

Laura's VCE year showcased her first film project which she wrote, directed, filmed and edited for her VCE, alongside a theatre performance, Letters for Lindy, which she also performed and directed. Laura was a member of HotHouse Theatre's Industry Co:Lab for emerging artists in 2021.

HER is Laura's debut acting in a professional production and she is grateful for all the support from her family and friends and excited about this opportunity.

IMOGEN KEEN
Set & Costume Design

Imogen has worked in professional stage design since the mid nineties. She has been designer-in-residence at The Street Theatre in Canberra since 2009, also designing for live performance, film media and installations for companies including COUP Canberra, Australian Dance Party, Urban Theatre Project, Jigsaw Theatre Company among others. In 2009, 2011 and 2018 Imogen received the Canberra Critics Circle Award for Theatre Design and in 2011 received the MEAA Peer Acknowledgement Award.

Recent works include *Twenty Minutes With The Devil* by Luis Gomez Romero & Desmond Manderson, *Art* by Yasmina Reza, *Breaking The Castle* by Peter Cook, *Flight Memory* by Alana Valentine and Sandra France, and Dylan Van Den Berg's *Ngadjung* and *Milk*.

Imogen's work is characterised by an inventive use of materials and objects and her involvement as a maker. Collaboration is at the core of her enduring interest in stage design as an integral part of theatre storytelling.

HELENA KERNAGHAN
Composer | Sound Design

Helena Kernaghan has established herself as one of the most versatile pianists and musicians of recent times. She has forged her own unique path in the Australian music scene from her hometown on the NSW-Victorian border Albury. Helena finished her master's in music performance at the University of Melbourne (VCA) in 2005 and has performed extensively throughout Australia and internationally. She is currently a member of the Orpheus Trio and has collaborated with Dutch thereminist Thorwald Jorgensen (Tempo Rubato,Melbourne), pianist Donna Coleman, clarinettist David Griffiths, tenor Shanul Sharma, & sopranos Merlyn Quaife & Ayse Goknur-Shana (Sydney Opera House).

Helena was the founding artistic director of the Albury Chamber Music Festival (2016-2019) and is currently the artistic director and CEO of Murray River Fine Music. Recent original works include a soundtrack for the children's story 'The River' for the 2021 Upstream Festival, providing a musical accompaniment for an abstract game of chess enacted by circus arts performers, and a sci-fi soundtrack for the short film 'Titanium'

ROB SCOTT
Lighting Design

Over many years Rob has worked in film and music production, photography, circus, theatre and education as well as building design and construction. Rob was Technical Operations Manager at HotHouse Theatre for 20 years.

His broad spectrum of experience and technical knowledge gives him a unique perspective on design and production for theatre and beyond. His hands-on approach has been applauded by Directors and Producers across Australia and internationally.

Highlights at HotHouse are set and lighting designs for *Parallax Island, Confidentially Yours, The Messiah, Australia! The Show!, The Laramie Project,* and lighting designs for *Second Childhood, A Midsummer Night's Dream, Such A Storm, Wonderlands, Olleanna, This is Where we Live* and *Between the Clouds.* Other credits include lighting designs for the Flying Fruit Fly Circus' *Stagefright ,Back in the Big Top* and *Time Flies,* A4 Circus Ensemble's *Downpour* and Casus' *Knee Deep,* and most recently *You & I* and *DnA.*

ANN-MAREE ELLIS
Movement Director

Ann-Maree began exploring dance improvisation in the 90s and was swept off her feet, literally, by Contact Improvisation (CI). Enamoured with improvised performance, she was nurtured by Melbourne's hotbed of practitioners including State of Flux, Trotman & Morrish, Al Wunder and Born in a Taxi. Internationally, she studied with the world's foremost exponent of CI, Nancy Stark Smith, improvisers K.J. Holmes and Julyen Hamilton, and companies Lower Left and SITI Company.

Ann-Maree was a founding member and performer of the dance improv collective, The Little Con, for 8 years. She taught the Dance Improvisation unit at Deakin University for 5 years. Her last significant performance was a 45-minute ensemble improvisation for Wodonga's *Everybody Dance Now* festival in 2013. Since 2012 she has coordinated Albury's *Write Around the Murray Festival*. She's excited to dust off the dance cobwebs and work on *HER*.

BECK PALMER
Producer

For over 30 years Beck has worked in performing arts for many companies and on innumerable productions. From volunteering in the scenic workshop of Ensemble Theatre, Sydney to training as a Stage Manager she really cut her teeth touring through Queensland, NSW, Victoria and overseas with Dancenorth Townsville - bringing performances and workshops to regional, national and international audiences and communities.

As Production Manager her highlights are: Chunky Move, REM Theatre, Marguerite Pepper Productions, Sydney Theatre Company, Soft Tread Productions, Sydney Festival, Adelaide Festival, Sydney Fringe, Bordeville Circus Festival, New Zealand Arts Festival, Wexford Opera Festival (Ireland), Brighton Comedy Festival (UK), Assembly Rooms (Edinburgh).

For HotHouse Theatre, Beck has liaised with producers, presenters, artists, audiences and organisations for all productions and programs since 2012. Beck is proud the company has leaned back into commissioning and producing work from regional artists, providing a platform for regional stories to be heard.

BEK GIBBS
Stage Manager

Bek Gibbs is a stage manager and producer with more than 10 years experience in theatre production. She has worked and toured regionally and internationally across a range of performance disciplines including circus, immersive theatre, arts festivals, community theatre and more.

Bek has honed her craft in organisations such as Broad Encounters, Circus OZ, the Melbourne International Comedy Festival, Crown Casino and Spiegelworld. She has a Bachelor of Production (Stage Management) from The Victorian College of the Arts. After establishing her career Bek returned to settle on the Border, now working as a freelance Stage Manager and Associate Producer at the Flying Fruit Fly Circus. Her passions lie in working with young people and her local community.

KOFI ISAACS
Production Manager

Kofi is a production manager and lighting designer based in Albury, NSW.

He is also a trained trapeze performer. His credits include, Design, *Those who Fall in Love like Anchors Dropped Upon the Ocean Floor* (HotHouse Theatre, The Butter Factory), *December* (Jake Silvestro, Ralph Wilson Theatre) *A Tale of Two Harpies* (Wilks & Bloom, The Butter Factory), *Tempo* (Flying Fruit Fly Circus, Sydney Opera House), *All the Shining Lights* (HotHouse Theatre, The Butter Factory). Production Management, *Neighbour* (Alyson Evans), *All the Shining Lights* (HotHouse Theatre), *HER* (HotHouse Theatre). Performance, Australian Circus Festival, Western Australian Circus Festival, Melbourne Fringe.

HANNAH MULHOLLAND
Production Assistant

Hannah Mulholland is passionate theatre technician and performer. She was Hothouse Theatre's technical trainee in 2022 to early 2023 studying her Certificate III in Live Production and Services.

She has been a production assistant on *This is Your City, Biting Dog Theatre Throwback, All the Shining Lights, Galah Bar Borderville* and *A Land of Snow and Ice.* She has also been the stage manager for *Embers staged reading* and *Bungambrawatha.*

Lauren Shepherd
Aerial Consultant

Lauren has been working as a professional performer and trainer in the circus industry for over 20 years and is currently working with the Flying Fruit fly Circus as a skills coach and facilitating their injury management and prevention programs.

Lauren was a student with the Flying Fruit fly Circus for 9 years and graduated in 2000. Since then, she has worked in independent circus productions, festivals, workshops, show creations, community outreach including remote communities, both nationally and internationally.

Lauren now resides in Albury with her family where she continues to pass on her circus knowledge. She is also a practicing Myotherapist.

HotHouse THEATRE

ABOUT HOTHOUSE THEATRE

For over 20 years, HotHouse Theatre has been creating and presenting artistic works on the Border region to enthusiastic audiences of all ages and backgrounds.

From humble beginnings as the Murray River Performance Group to standing strong as one of the last remaining professional theatre companies in regional Australia, HotHouse has a rich and celebrated history of commissioning, producing, nurturing and presenting new, contemporary Australian theatre within a vibrant regional setting.

HotHouse Theatre incubates, makes and presents 100% Australian theatre, divergent in form and voice, that speaks to our region and the nation.

We invest in regional professional practice. We collaborate with artists, locally and nationally, to engage and inspire audiences. We inspire insight into our humanity through creative investigations that reflect the world around us. Through shared experiences, we stimulate the imagination of the region.

CELSIUS: INDEPENDENT THEATRE PROGRAM

The origins of *HER* began in 2019 as *Heart Story*, in the first year of HotHouse Theatre's CELSIUS: Independent Theatre program.

CELSIUS supports the development of local, independent theatre practitioners through creative development and presentation of theatre works that ignite and inspire regional audiences.

Heart Story was one of the first CELSIUS creative developments and its evolution into *HER* is one of the program's great success stories. *Heart Story* was developed by Kerryn Beatty with Suzanne Pereira as Director, Alyson Evans as Dramaturg and Helena Kernaghan as Composer. We acknowledge the valuable contribution of these artists to the journey of *HER*.

HOTHOUSE THEATRE STAFF

Artistic Director & CEO	Karla Conway
Business Manager	Madeleine Schnelle
Producer	Beck Palmer
Associate Producer – First Nations	Tiffany Ward
Programs Coordinator	Clancy Hauser
Associate Artist	Rachel McNamara
Communications	Luke Preston
Venue & Technical Manager	Kofi Isaacs
Technical Trainee	Hannah Mulholland

ACKNOWLEDGMENTS

HotHouse Theatre gratefully acknowledges the support of our Government Funders:

Australian Government RISE Fund   CREATIVE VICTORIA   NSW GOVERNMENT   CITY OF WODONGA VIC   AlburyCity